ROCKY MOUNTAIN ADVENTURE

© WAGNER & TELDON PUBLISHING, 1986

ISBN 0-88668-052-2

Published by
WAGNER & TELDON PUBLISHING LTD.
58 West 6th Ave.
Vancouver, B.C. V5Y 1K1

Typeset by
PEREGRINE PRESS
White Rock, B.C.

Printed by
WAGNER & TELDON PUBLISHING LTD.
Vancouver, B.C.

ROCKY MOUNTAIN ADVENTURE

Text by Audrey Fraggalosch

 Wagner & Teldon Publishing, Vancouver, Canada, 1986

At night the lights of the Banff townsite cast a warm glow over the surrounding mountain slopes.

Moraine Lake and the Valley of the Ten Peaks in Banff are one of the most popular scenic and recreation areas of the Rocky Mountain parks.

CONTENTS

HIGH ADVENTURE

The magic of the Rockies is undeniable. In this magnificent mountain world, you can view alpine scenery at its finest, canoe in crystalline lakes, hike through flower-strewn meadows, or ski the freshest, deepest powder in Canada. The less adventurous can enjoy innumerable scenic viewpoints from the car window, relax in bubbling, mineral hot springs, browse the quaint gift shops and galleries, or simply luxuriate in the elegant accommodations of Banff Springs Hotel, Chateau Lake Louise, or Jasper Park Lodge.

The Rockies are part of a great mountain system called the Western Cordillera which runs the full length of North and South America. Millions of years ago, the Rockies were formed when layers of rock from the seabed were pushed up by titanic volcanic forces acting beneath the earth's crust. As the crust rose, it became folded and broken, and eventually, a rugged strip of mountain ranges was created. During subsequent ages, immense glaciers advanced and retreated, carving out broad, flat valleys, and grinding mountain peaks into their dramatic present-day shapes. Water from the melting ice then filled valley lakes and river basins. A remnant of the glaciers of the last of these great ice ages can be seen at the Columbia Icefields, located 125 kilometres north of Lake Louise.

Visitors to the Rockies are sure to be impressed with the unspoiled forests which blanket the mountain slopes. You will notice a change in the types of vegetation as you travel higher into the mountains. At lower elevations the hillsides are covered with taller, thicker trees such as Englemann spruce, western red cedar, and Douglas-fir. Higher up, trees, such as alpine fir and white spruce, become smaller and have a spire-like form which helps them shed heavy snowfalls. At timberline conditions are too harsh for normal tree growth, and the mountain sides open to rolling meadows. Burdened with snow for most of the

⟫ The picturesque Opabin Plateau is located in the Lake O'Hara region of Yoho National Park.

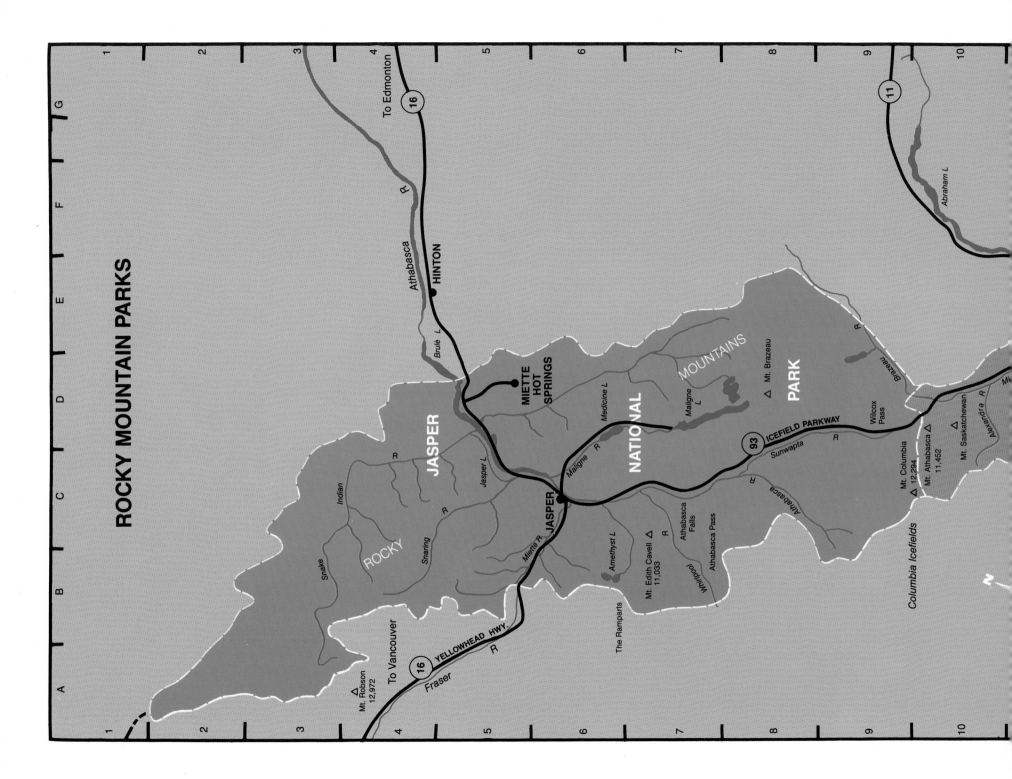

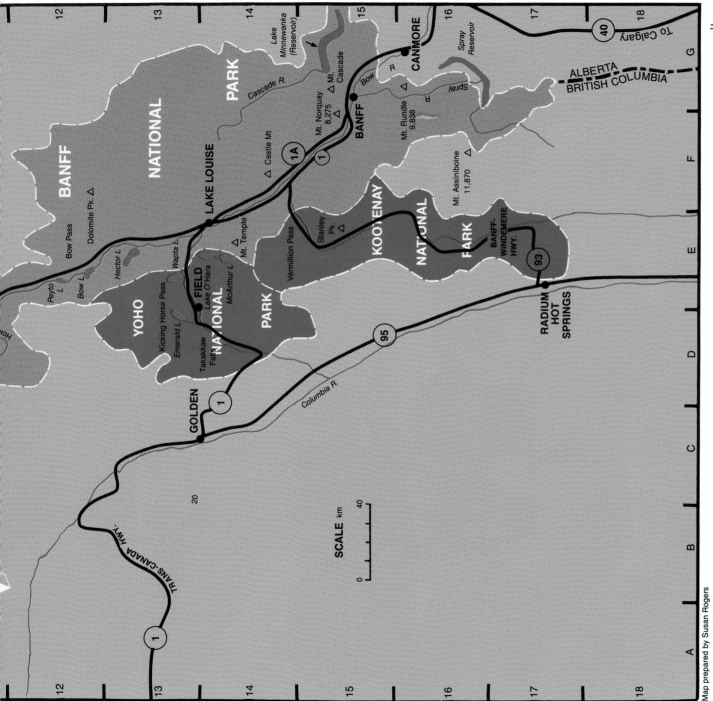

SPECIAL ATTRACTIONS

JASPER NATIONAL PARK

Mt. Robson	4A
Jasper Lake	5C
Athabasca Falls	7C
Jasper Townsite	6C
Columbia Icefield	9B
Maligne Lake	7D

BANFF NATIONAL PARK

Banff Townsite	15G
Mt. Athabasca	10D
Mt. Rundle	16G

YOHO & KOOTENAY NATIONAL PARKS

Takakkaw Falls	14D
Radium Hot Springs	17E
Emerald Lake	13D
Lake O'Hara	14E

Map prepared by Susan Rogers

year, the alpine meadows explode with an incredible profusion of colourful blossoms during the short summer season. The alpine gardens give way to barren ice and rock pinnacles on the mountain peaks.

Wildlife is abundant in the Rockies. Deer and elk graze in forest openings and alpine meadows on tender grasses and herbs. Moose browse knee-deep along the edge of lakes and marshes where they feed on aquatic plants, especially water lilies. At higher elevations, mountain sheep and goats roam the ridges and rock outcrops. Black bear and grizzly range throughout the forest zones, being particularly abundant during the summer in shrubby areas, berry patches, and in lush alpine meadows. The most conspicuous birds of the mountain parks are the ubiquitous ravens whose croaking calls echo through the valleys, and the grey jays and Clark's nutcrackers that shadow the mountain hiker in hopes of a handout. Mountain lakes are enlivened by a variety of colourful waterfowl as well as gulls, grebes, and loons.

The value of this magnificent wilderness was first recognized officially by the Canadian government through an act of Parliament in 1885 which set aside for all time the unspoiled beauty of the Banff area. In subsequent years, Jasper, Yoho, and Kootenay were added to the Rocky Mountain park system. Today there are many national and provincial parks in the Rockies. Set aside to protect the natural landscape and wildlife, these lands are for present and future generations to enjoy. Waiting for you is a Rocky Mountain adventure you'll never forget!

❮ Mountain goats inhabit the steepest, rockiest terrain possible.
⌃ The broad valley of the Athabasca River was an early fur trading route.

JASPER
Wilderness Preserved

Jasper is the largest and most northerly of the adjoining mountain parks. Encompassing an area of over 6750 square kilometres, it lies along the eastern slope of the Rockies and is bounded on the south by Banff National Park. Established in 1907, the park has a colourful history of intrepid explorers, hardy fur traders, determined government surveyors, and pioneering railway development. Many of the present day hiking trails were once important trading routes for trappers and prospectors, such as the famous Athabasca Trail.

Jasper is primarily a wilderness park. A remote and rugged mountain expanse, here outdoor enthusiasts can ski, white-water canoe, or hike in uncrowded conditions. Maligne Lake, the largest glacial lake in the Canadian Rockies, Mount Columbia which soars to over 3700 metres, and the rushing Athabasca waterfalls are a few of the magnificent attractions. The park is a haven for wildlife—moose, elk, mule deer, black and grizzly bears, coyote, and bighorn sheep. Many species can be seen directly from the road, while others, like mountain goats and grizzlies, inhabit the isolated high country where only the most adventuresome hikers choose to wander.

Located 360 kilometres west of Edmonton, Jasper can be reached from the south via the Banff-Jasper Highway, from the east via the Edmonton-Jasper Highway, and from the west via the Yellowhead Highway. The park is also serviced by railway and air transportation. The Jasper townsite is a small but active resort complete with a golf course, tennis courts, and recreation centre, as well as the park's information bureau and administration buildings.

》 *Elk are found throughout Jasper National Park and are most likely to be seen feeding in alpine meadows early in the morning.*

》》 *The Columbia Icefield Chalet is situated at an elevation of 2135 metres in a region of high peaks and glaciers. It is accessible from the Columbia Icefields Parkway.*

⌢ *The aerial tramway provides visitors with a panoramic view of the Jasper townsite and the Athabasca River Valley.*

❮ *Maligne Canyon is one of the most advanced pothole canyons in North America.*

❮❮ *Jasper Park Lodge on beautiful Lac Beauvert is not just a hotel, but a self-contained village accommodating approximately 550 people.*

> Mount Robson is the highest peak in the Canadian Rockies at 3954 metres. It is located just outside the boundary of Jasper National Park in British Columbia.

> Mountain climbers test their skill and sense of adventure in the precipitous terrain.

⌃ *Cavell Lake is one of the best locations for spectacular close-up photos of Mount Edith Cavell.*

≫ *Common golden-eye ducks nest in cavities of trees along the shores of mountain lakes.*

≪ Raccoons are nocturnal inhabitants of the mountain parks. They forage along streams and lakesides for shellfish, frogs, and other small animals.

♡ Columbian ground squirrels dig their burrows in the sub-alpine regions of Jasper National Park.

≪≪ The Ramparts are massive mountain formations with remarkable folds, upheavals, and faults visible in the rock strata.

≪ *Emerald-green Maligne Lake, the largest glacial lake in the Canadian Rockies, is 27 kilometres long with over 80 kilometres of shoreline.*

≫ *The combined waters of the Athabasca and Sunwapta Rivers cascade 22 metres over Athabasca Falls.*

BANFF
Mountain Heartland

Located in the heart of the Canadian Rockies, Banff is Canada's oldest and most heavily utilized national park. It was originally set aside in 1885 to preserve mineral hot springs for public use, and now has become one of North America's most popular holiday spots. Campgrounds, resorts, downhill and cross-country skiing facilities, and 1100 kilometres of hiking trails are contained within the park's 4000 square kilometres.

Banff's many mountains, lakes, and valleys offer some of the finest and most varied camping and backpacking experiences in the Rockies. One of the most famous hiking areas is Lake Louise, an emerald of fresh water surrounded by towering mountains and snowfields. Visitors can stay at Chateau Lake Louise, an exquisite old hotel which stands atop the glacial moraine that dams the lake. Mount Assiniboine, the Matterhorn of the Rockies, is also popular with climbers and sightseers alike. Visible for many miles in all directions, it soars over 3600 metres into the crystalline mountain air.

Located 120 kilometres west of Calgary, the town of Banff is well serviced by highways, railways, and air flights. The townsite is a year-round resort and cultural centre, with a variety of facilities including the famous Banff Springs Hotel, the world-class Banff School of Fine Arts, the park information centre, a natural history museum, and a delight to bathers, the old, mineral hotsprings at the base of Sulphur Mountain.

〉 *Cascade Mountain towers over Banff Avenue.*

〉〉 *Mount Rundle, lying southeast of Banff, dominates the skyline of this quaint mountain town.*

Lake Minnewanka, meaning "lake of the water spirit", is the largest lake in Banff National Park

≫ *Usually secretive and nocturnal, the mountain lion is seldom seen by park visitors.*

≫≫ *Mount Temple (3548 metres) is one of the highest peaks in the southern Canadian Rockies.*

▷ The red squirrel, a lively and noisy rodent, is found throughout the mountain forests.

⌃ The saw-whet owl, a tiny bird of prey, inhabits coniferous forests where it hunts small birds.

◁ Castle Mountain is one of Canada's best examples of "castellate" mountains.

‹ Chipmunks are found throughout
the mountain parks, delighting
visitors with their scampering
antics.

› This is an aerial view of the Banff
townsite as seen from Sulphur
Mountain. A cable car takes visitors
to the summit.

Canada's Matterhorn, Mount Assiniboine (3617 metres), is one of the highest peaks in Banff National Park.

A hiker exults in his conquest of the summit of Mount Assiniboine.

◁ Bow Lake with Bow Peak in the background, is a favourite canoeing area.

▷ Grizzly bears are the largest and most dangerous animals in the Rocky Mountains, especially if encountered by surprise. Hikers should wear bells to warn bears of their approach.

《《 Glacier, or avalanche, lilies are among the first flowers to bloom in the alpine meadows.

《⌃ The spectacular blossoms of red monkey flowers attract hummingbirds into the alpine.

《⌄ For a few weeks each summer, the alpine meadows explode with a kaleidoscope of blooms.

⌃ Moist soils near mountain streams usually support a thick growth of alpine flowers.

⌄ Red Indian paintbrush and blue lupine are two of the most common alpine blooms.

≪ North America's most powerful owl, the great horned, terrorizes the night-time forests in search of skunks, porcupines, and varying hares.

⌃ The pika, or rock rabbit, inhabits rock-cluttered alpine slopes. It gathers grasses, dries them in the sun, and stores them underground for winter use.

≫ Originally built in 1888, the Banff Springs Hotel still charms its year-round guests.

≪ The emerald waters of Lake Louise are ideal for a summer's paddle.

♡ Chateau Lake Louise is an elegant, old hotel that accommodates over 700 guests.

≪ Lake Louise, named after Princess Louise, the daughter of Queen Victoria and the wife of Canada's Governor General, the Marquis of Lorne, is one of the most popular resort areas in the Rockies.

YOHO–KOOTENAY
Places of Wonder

Yoho and Kootenay are two adjoining parks situated on the western slope of the Rockies in British Columbia. Both parks claim some of the most scenic and challenging mountain terrain in western Canada.

Yoho is a Cree Indian word meaning "awe"—an apt name for this spectacular park. Its natural wonders include Canada's highest waterfalls (the Takakkaw), towering mountain peaks, crystal caves, and exceptional Hoodoo formations. The park contains many excellent hiking areas with the most popular trails being in the vicinity of Lake O'Hara and the Yoho Valley.

Kootenay National Park boasts its own breath-taking wilderness attractions including steep canyons, spectacular waterfalls and mineral hot springs. The Banff-Windermere Highway, the first motor road constructed across the central Rockies, runs through the park allowing easy backcountry access, with trails radiating from both sides of the road.

Visitor access to Yoho is by the western section of the Trans-Canada Highway as well as the Canadian Pacific Railway. Kootenay Park is reached from the northeast via the Trans-Canada Highway and from the south via Highway 95. The Banff-Windermere Highway connects these two routes. Most tourist services for these two parks can be found in nearby towns. The Field townsite services Yoho National Park, while Radium Junction, Invermere, and Athalmer are close to Kootenay National Park. Special tourist facilities in Yoho include a small chalet at Lake O'Hara (reservations only), and in Kootenay, the Radium Hot Springs complex, a natural mineral bath.

⟫ *The Elizabeth Parker hut, with Mount Odaray in the background, is a popular refuge for hikers.*

❮ *The grey jay, or whiskey jack, is fearless of man and often alights on picnic tables in quest of a handout.*

❤ *Rocky Mountain bighorn sheep live in herds near, or above, timberline.*

⌃ *Hoary marmots are the largest members of the squirrel family, weighing up to 13 kilograms.*

⌄ *Usually solitary, black bears come together during the mating season and occasionally when feeding in berry patches.*

⟩ *Mount Burgess towers above Emerald Lake in Yoho National Park.*

McArthur Lake is named after the first white man to see the O'Hara region. Surrounded by mountain peaks and lying at 2246 metres, it is a short hike from the O'Hara Cabin.

This natural bridge in the Rockies is located near Mount Stephen.

《《 *Lake O'Hara is the jewel of the Rockies, a beautiful, glacial lake surrounded by snowy mountain peaks.*

⌃ *The castellate blocks of Cathedral Mountain (3189 metres) dominate the skyline.*

《 *Takkakaw Falls is the highest waterfall in Canada.*

∧ Rose hips, the fruits of wild roses, are food for many birds and animals.

∨ Chanterelles are delicious, edible mushrooms that grow in sub-alpine regions in the autumn.

< Elk with velvet antlers are frequently spotted on the roadsides during late summer.

> Found throughout the Rocky Mountain parks, bobcats are small, powerful predators that hunt game birds, hares, mice, and other rodents.

❯ *Lake O'Hara and St. Mary's Lake attract visitors from around the world.*

❮ Although the wolf is seldom seen, the sounds of the howling wolf pack sometimes serenade the camps of wilderness backpackers.

❮❮ The Opabin Plateau near Lake O'Hara is covered with a network of hiking trails.

≪ The largest members of the deer family, moose are frequently seen feeding on aquatic plants along mountain lakeshores and marshes.

≫ Larches are the only conifers that change colour and lose their needles each fall. Here they cast a golden glow on this stretch of the Continental Divide.

Soaking in the mineral hot springs at Radium is a wonderful way to relax muscles tired from hiking.

The stillness of a winter morning in the mountains is reflected in the
waters of Wapta Lake near Field, British Columbia.

⌃ Ski-touring is an exciting way to explore pristine winter slopes in the mountains.

‹ Mountain climbers are a breed apart! They thrill to the challenge of an untried peak.

‹‹ Peculiar Peak's distinctive shape makes it a well-known landmark in Yoho National Park.

The Eiffel Lake trail leads hikers to one of the most remote areas of Banff National Park.